Natural Disasters

Tornadoes

Louise Park

Smart Apple Media

This edition first published in 2008 in the United States of America by Smart Apple Media.

Smart Apple Media
2140 Howard Drive West
North Mankato, Minnesota 56003

First published in 2007 by
MACMILLAN EDUCATION AUSTRALIA PTY LTD
627 Chapel Street, South Yarra, Australia 3141

Visit our Web site at www.macmillan.com.au or go directly to www.macmillanlibrary.com.au

Associated companies and representatives throughout the world.

Library of Congress Cataloging-in-Publication Data

Park, Louise, 1961-
   Tornadoes / by Louise Park.
   p. cm. – (Natural disasters)
   Includes index.
   ISBN 978-1-59920-114-6
1. Tornadoes–Juvenile literature. 2. Natural disasters–Juvenile literature. I. Title.

   QC955.2.P37 2007
   551.55'3–dc22

                                                       2007004660

Edited by Sam Munday and Erin Richards
Text and cover design by Ivan Finnegan, iF design
Page layout by Ivan Finnegan, iF design
Photo research by Jes Senbergs
Illustrations by Andy Craig and Nives Porcellato, pp. 6, 7, 10
Maps by designscope, pp. 8, 12, 16, 24

Printed in U.S.

Acknowledgements
The author and the publisher are grateful to the following for permission to reproduce copyright material:
Front cover photograph: car escaping from Oklahoma tornado, May 1999, courtesy of AAP/AP Photo/J. Pat Carter.

Background textures courtesy of Ivan Finnegan, iF design.

AAP/AP Photo/J. Pat Carter, pp. 1, 13 (bottom); AAP/AP Photo/Fred Stewart, p. 24; Bettmann/Corbis, p. 25; Andrea Booher/ FEMA News Photo, p. 28; Chicago Historic Museum, p. 21; Gary Crabbe/Alamy, p. 11; Jeff Greenberg/Alamy, p. 22; William T. Hark, pp. 16, 17; Hulton Archive/Topical Press Agency/Getty Images, p. 9; NOAA, pp. 4, 8, 13 (top), 14, 15 (both), 18, 20; Photolibrary, pp. 26, 27, 29; Joel Sartore/Getty Images, p. 19; A. T. Willett/Alamy, p. 5.

Contents

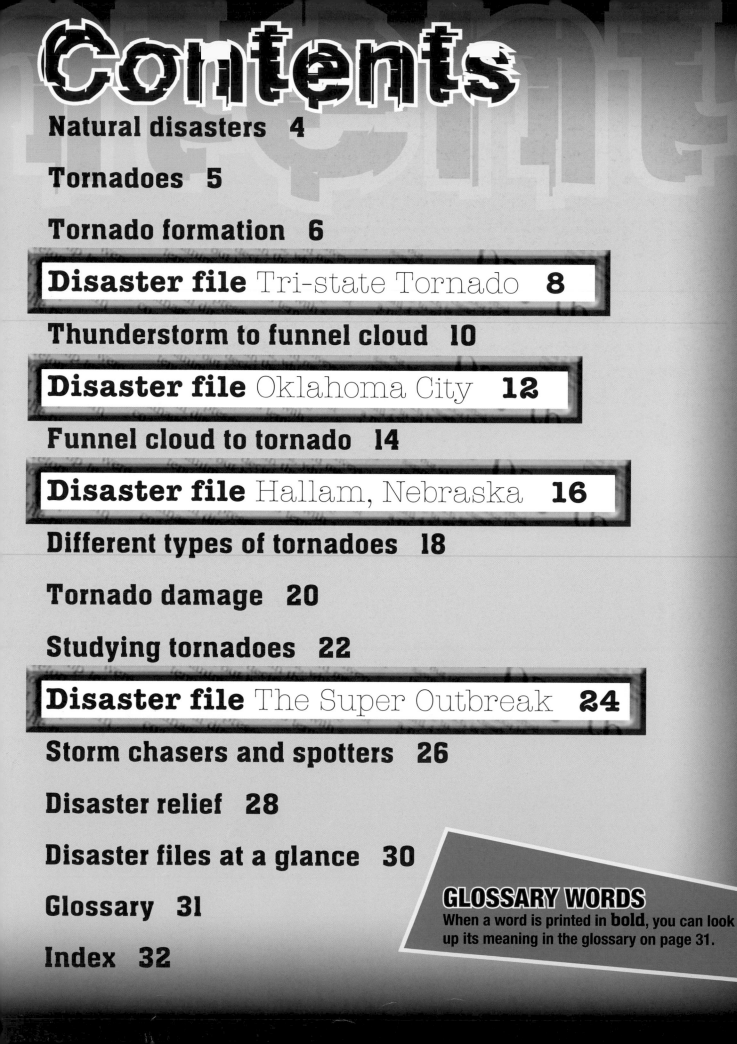

GLOSSARY WORDS

When a word is printed in **bold**, you can look up its meaning in the glossary on page 31.

Natural disasters

Natural disasters are events that occur naturally. They are not caused by human action. They can happen all over the world at any time. When natural disasters occur in populated areas, they can result in death, injury, and damage to property.

Types of natural disasters

There are many types of natural disasters, such as tornadoes, wildfires, droughts, and earthquakes. Each type occurs for very different reasons and affects Earth in different ways. Although they are different, they all create chaos and bring **devastation** and destruction with them wherever they strike.

Tornadoes are sometimes called twisters.

Tornadoes

Tornadoes are violent windstorms that can spin at enormous speeds. They are one of the world's recurring natural disasters.

What is a tornado?

Tornadoes are twisting columns of air that make contact with the ground. They form within thunderclouds and appear to hang down from them in an upside-down cone shape. Sometimes tornadoes are called twisters because the column of air twists around and around with such enormous power.

Where do tornadoes happen?

Tornadoes can occur anywhere on Earth if the conditions are right, but most tornadoes occur in the middle of the United States. The states of Texas, Oklahoma, Illinois, and Missouri are part of an area known as Tornado Alley, where the conditions are ideal for tornadoes.

DID YOU KNOW?
The most tornadoes in one season happened in 1992 in the U.S. A total of 1,293 tornadoes touched down in that season.

Any buildings in the path of a tornado are in danger of being damaged or destroyed.

Tornado formation

Tornadoes form inside dark thunderclouds that are heavy with rain. These clouds are created as part of Earth's water cycle. When these heavy thunderclouds combine with winds, conditions are right for a tornado to form.

The water cycle

Thunderclouds are created as part of Earth's natural water cycle. As the sun and warm air heat Earth, water **evaporates** into **water vapor**. Water vapor is an invisible gas that rises up into the **atmosphere.** As the vapor rises, it cools, collects, and **condenses** into water droplets to form clouds. When large thunderclouds join together, they can unleash enormous amounts of rain. It is when tornadoes form inside these thunderclouds that damage can be caused.

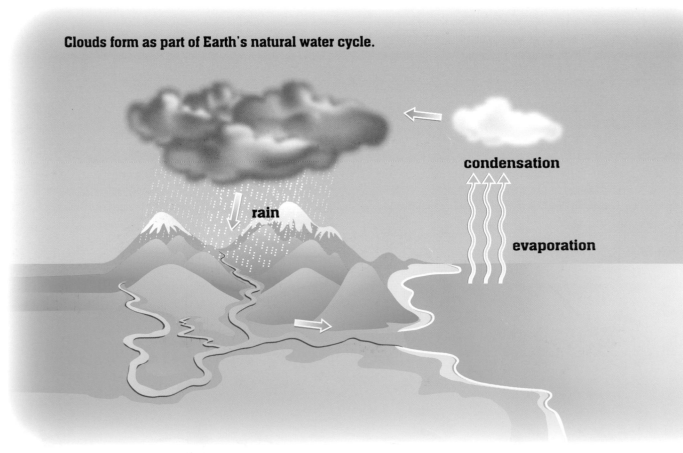

Clouds form as part of Earth's natural water cycle.

condensation

rain

evaporation

Wind

Wind is caused by air moving from cool, dry areas and warm, **humid** areas. These are known as **high pressure areas** and **low pressure areas**. When a lot of warm, humid air rises from a low pressure area, it causes cooler, high pressure air to rush in and fill the space. When the exchange of air is small, it creates a gentle breeze. When a large amount of low pressure air pulls upward from Earth, it creates an **updraft**. When this happens, a downdraft of high pressure air rushes rapidly into the space. This rapid rush of wind is what gives a tornado its power. For a tornado to form there needs to be a great deal of movement between these areas of cool and warm air.

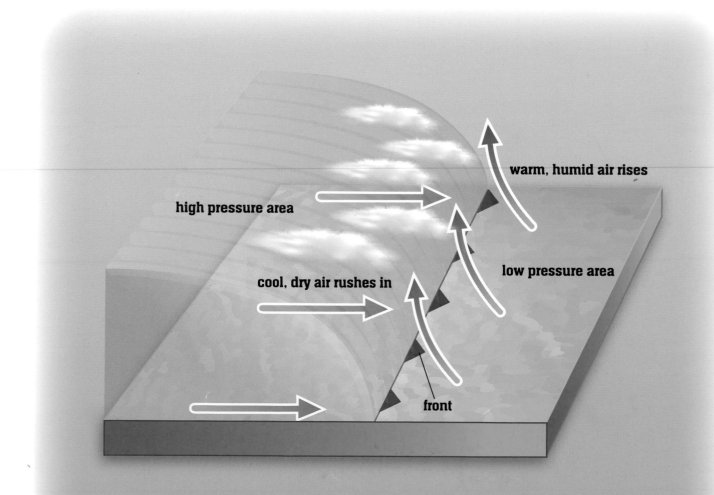

warm, humid air rises

high pressure area

low pressure area

cool, dry air rushes in

front

The place where a low pressure area meets a high pressure area is known as a front.

DISASTER FILE
Tri-state Tornado

WHAT	The deadliest tornado in the history of the U.S.
WHERE	Tornado Alley in the states of Missouri, Illinois, and Indiana
WHEN	March 18, 1925
FUJITA SCALE	F5

The Tri-state Tornado was rated F5 on the **Fujita scale**. It moved with a ground speed of 73 miles (117 km) an hour, making it the fastest forward-moving major tornado.

Why did it happen?

Meteorologists have studied the weather patterns on the day the Tri-state Tornado struck. That morning, the weather was ideal for tornado-making. There was a significant surface of low pressure over northwest Arkansas, southwest and southeast Missouri, southern Illinois, and southwest Indiana. It built and moved, reaching eastern Indiana that evening. This allowed enormous amounts of warm, moist air from the Gulf of Mexico to move into the tri-state area. This large exchange of air created the sucking, spiraling winds that formed this tornado.

People hoped their homes would not be in the deadly tornado's path.

Counting the cost

This tornado left a continuous track of 219 miles (352 km). Beginning in Missouri, the tornado crossed the Mississippi river into Illinois where it did most of its damage. The mile-wide funnel destroyed the town of Gorham and devastated a number of other towns. Within 40 minutes, it had killed over 600 people and left over 1,000 injured. After crossing into Indiana, it took the lives of at least another 70 people. It traveled another 10 miles (16 km) before it died out.

The death toll is believed to be 695 with a total of 2,027 people injured. The tornado lasted about three and a half hours. During that time, three states, 19 counties, and nearly 20 communities were affected.

Many were left homeless after the tornado destroyed their houses.

Thunderstorm to funnel cloud

Funnel clouds form when thunderstorms and fast winds interact. Before a thunderstorm develops, there is a change in wind direction and wind speed. As the wind climbs higher and higher, it changes direction and gathers speed. This creates an invisible, horizontal spinning motion in the lower atmosphere. Warm, humid air gets sucked up into the thunderclouds. Cooler air rushes rapidly into the space that is left. The rising air updraft tilts the spinning air from horizontal to vertical.

The spinning wind begins to drop down from the cloud as more air is sucked into the funnel that is forming. This column of air, known as a funnel cloud, starts to lengthen. Inside it, water vapor starts to condense. This creates heavy, dark clouds that rise up inside the funnel cloud. When the spinning wind is powerful enough, the column eventually reaches the ground. When a funnel cloud touches the ground, it becomes a tornado.

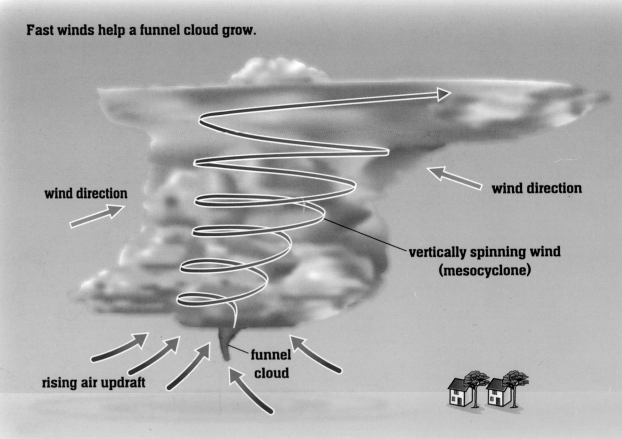

Fast winds help a funnel cloud grow.

wind direction

wind direction

vertically spinning wind (mesocyclone)

rising air updraft

funnel cloud

Tornado-forming thunderstorms

Tornadoes do not form in all thunderstorms. Most thunderstorms are fairly small and not strong enough to produce tornadoes. Only **supercell thunderstorms** are large and powerful enough to produce devastating tornadoes.

Supercell thunderstorms

A supercell is a severe thunderstorm with a deep, rotating updraft. Supercells are the largest and most severe class of thunderstorm. They can produce large amounts of hail, heavy rainfall, and strong winds. About one third of all supercell thunderstorms produce tornadoes.

The spinning winds inside supercells are called mesocyclones. Some of these winds die out, while others spin so fast that they create funnel clouds. The strongest and most dangerous tornadoes form in the updraft area of mesocyclones. Supercells regularly occur in Tornado Alley.

Supercell thunderstorms can produce deadly tornadoes.

DISASTER FILE
Oklahoma City

WHAT	The most expensive tornado in the world
WHERE	Oklahoma, U.S.
WHEN	May 3, 1999
FUJITA SCALE	F5

The Oklahoma tornado outbreak took place on May 3, 1999. During this outbreak, 66 tornadoes were created in Oklahoma and Kansas. Many of these tornadoes rated F5 on the Fujita scale. The tornadoes created havoc for three days.

Why did it happen?

The outbreak was created from multiple supercell thunderstorms. On May 3, a high risk warning was issued. This warned people that the developing thunderstorm could create deadly tornadoes. The thunderstorms continued into the afternoon, and later that evening tornadoes broke out. The supercell thunderstorms produced a tornado with the strongest winds ever recorded. A **Doppler radar** measured the winds inside this tornado at 317.5 miles (511 km) an hour.

Counting the cost

The tornado that hit Oklahoma City killed 36 people and destroyed more than 10,000 buildings. In the two days that followed this deadly tornado, many other tornadoes struck. Several of these tornadoes measured between F3 and F4 and also caused significant damage. The Oklahoma outbreaks destroyed approximately 2,000 homes and damaged another 6,500.

The damage to Oklahoma City cost $1.1 billion.

A car manages to escape one of the Oklahoma tornadoes.

DID YOU KNOW?

Between 700–1,000 tornadoes occur every year in the U.S. Sixty-three tornadoes once struck Arkansas on one single day. This is the highest number of tornadoes ever recorded in one day.

Funnel cloud to tornado

Funnel clouds are spinning columns of air that hang from the base of the cloud. Not all funnel clouds reach the ground. When they do, at a moment known as "touchdown," they become tornadoes. Every tornado begins life as a funnel cloud. Funnel clouds look like cones that extend out from the base of the cloud. They frequently form during supercell thunderstorms.

Some tornadoes have more than one funnel. Smaller funnels can form inside the wall of the central funnel. Tornado funnels can range in width from just 10 feet (3 m) to as much as 1 mile (1.6 km).

Think about it

Tornado funnels are usually between 33 and 1,312 feet (10 and 400 m) wide. The Tri-state Tornado funnel was nearly one mile (1.6 km) wide.

This might look like a tornado, but the funnel cloud has not touched down yet.

Touching down

As funnels stretch down closer to the ground, their winds pick up dirt, rock, and **debris**. The more dirt that is sucked up into the funnel, the darker the funnel becomes. It can also become very noisy when it touches down. This is due to all the dirt, rock, and debris spinning around in the strong, whirling winds.

Not all funnel clouds become tornadoes.

DID YOU KNOW?
Some tornadoes are invisible. They can be hidden by clouds that are so low they hide the funnel. Sometimes there is no cloud in the funnel. When this happens, we just see the dust and debris but no funnel.

A funnel cloud touches down and forms a tornado.

DISASTER FILE
Hallam, Nebraska

WHAT	The widest tornado on record
WHERE	Nebraska, U.S.
WHEN	May 22, 2004
FUJITA SCALE	F4

The tornado that struck Nebraska in 2004 engulfed the town of Hallam. By the time it reached the town, the tornado's funnel was 2.5 miles (4 km) wide. The Hallam tornado left a path of devastation more than 52 miles (84 km) long. It touched down for nearly 100 minutes.

Why did it happen?

Nebraska is considered to be part of Tornado Alley. This area is the perfect breeding ground for storms that produce tornadoes. The Hallam tornado was born out of a supercell thunderstorm. Weather conditions were perfect for winds within the mesocyclone to build.

Residents of Russell, Kansas, received a tornado warning when this supercell developed in Tornado Alley, just days before the Hallam tornado struck.

Counting the cost

Because the tornado was so wide, most of Hallam was completely destroyed. Buildings were flattened, hopper cars had been tossed from a freight train, and vehicles had been rolled. Many farms and rural land also suffered extensive damage and destruction. Despite this tornado being the widest on record, it only killed one person and injured 37.

Think about it

The Hallam tornado touched down for 100 minutes and destroyed most of the town. One tornado that touched down in 1977 lasted more than seven hours.

Cars were flipped and buildings destroyed by the force of the Hallam tornado.

Different types of tornadoes

Different types of tornadoes can be formed depending on the type of terrain they travel over. Waterspouts form over water, and dust devils form in hot, dry areas.

Waterspouts

When tornadoes form over water, they are called waterspouts. As a tornado passes over a lake or the sea, its funnel touches the surface of the water and sucks it up. At the base of the funnel, the wind can whip the water into big waves. Although waterspouts are not as powerful as land tornadoes, they can still do amazing things. Waterspouts have picked up boats and even jetties. They can suck out the entire contents of ponds and, if they reach land, destroy buildings. Waterspouts do not usually last more than 30 minutes.

Waterspouts travel slowly and appear as dark tubes of water.

Dust devils

Dust devils, or whirlwinds, are similar to tornadoes but are formed differently. Dust devils form in hot, dry areas, usually under clear skies. As the ground heats up, hot air rises and more air rushes into the space that is created. As more hot air rises, a spinning effect is created. Dust devils are rarely attached to a cloud and always begin on the ground. They tend to travel through desert areas. They may be small and just last a few minutes or they can become huge funnels that last for hours.

DID YOU KNOW?
Dust devils have different names in different places. In Australia, they are known as Willy Willies.

Dust devils occur on hot days and do not have the power of a tornado.

Tornado damage

Although tornadoes do not travel very fast, they can be very destructive. The damage they cause is because of wind speed and suction, flying debris, and air pressure.

Wind speed and suction

The speed of the winds twisting in a tornado funnel can be more than 300 miles (483 km) an hour. Winds at this speed can destroy everything in their path. Sometimes the path of a tornado is narrow and clearly marked. When this happens, the damage is confined to a small strip. At other times, the damage can be much wider than the width of the funnel.

The winds inside a tornado funnel spin upward and suck debris up with them. The faster the winds spin, the more sucking power a tornado has. Tornadoes can be strong enough to lift roofs, cars, trees, and even whole buildings. These objects can be carried for some time before they are thrown out in all directions.

The winds of a tornado can flatten everything in their path.

Flying debris

The objects thrown from a tornado are known as flying debris. Flying debris can be thrown at incredibly high speeds. Debris can be all sorts of shapes and sizes. Rocks, clothing, trees, parts of cars, and even the surface of roads have all been sucked up and thrown out by tornadoes. Both large and small debris can be destructive. Large items, such as fridges, have been thrown onto people and homes. Smaller items, such as straw, have been found driven into tree trunks like darts. At high speeds, even sand and gravel can be deadly.

Air pressure

A tornado produces sudden changes in air pressure. Inside a tornado, the air pressure is very low. The air pressure inside houses and buildings on the ground is normal. When a tornado passes over a building, it causes the air pressure inside it to expand violently. This change in pressure can blow out windows and doors and can even cause a house to explode within seconds.

During the 1925 Tri-state Tornado, this house was picked up and dropped 59 feet (18 m) from its foundation.

Studying tornadoes

Meteorologists are scientists who study and predict the weather. Although tornadoes can be hard to predict, meteorologists continue to study and measure them. They look for better ways to predict whether a tornado is going to form.

Predicting tornadoes

Because tornadoes build inside thunderstorms, meteorologists do not always know they are there. They are not like hurricanes, which can be seen building into dangerous storms. Tornadoes can build and then touch down in less than 10 minutes. This does not allow much time to warn people, so when severe thunderstorms develop, meteorologists watch for tornadoes. When a tornado is spotted, alerts are broadcast as quickly as possible.

Meteorologists uses satellites to collect information about the weather.

Measuring tools

Meteorologists regularly use tools, such as **anemometers**, to measure wind speeds. However, anemometers cannot be used to measure tornadoes. The winds inside tornadoes are twisting at such high speed that anemometers would be destroyed in the funnels. Instead, a Doppler radar is used, since it does not need to be placed inside the tornado. A Doppler radar sends out radio waves from an antenna to gather information about wind movement and speed.

The Fujita scale

The Fujita scale, or F scale, is used to measure the intensity of a tornado. It looks at the damage and destruction caused by a tornado and calculates the force needed to produce this sort of damage. The F scale rating F3 indicates a "severe twister." F3 tornadoes are capable of destroying wooden buildings, and can lift roofs and walls from other structures. F5 tornadoes are the strongest on the scale. They can rip up roads and concrete surfaces.

FUJITA SCALE

Scale	Wind Speed	Potential damage	Description
F0	less than 72 miles (116 km) an hour	minimal	• some damage to chimneys • branches broken off trees • damage to road signs and billboards
F1	72–112 miles (116–180 km) an hour	moderate	• tiles torn off roofs • mobile homes overturned • cars pushed off the road
F2	113–155 miles (181–250 km) an hour	considerable	• roofs torn off houses • mobile homes destroyed • cars rolled, light objects thrown some distance
F3	156–205 miles (251–330 km) an hour	severe	• roofs and some walls torn off well-built houses • trains overturned • most trees uprooted
F4	206–257 miles (331–415 km) an hour	extreme	• well-built houses destroyed • structures with weak foundations blown away • cars and other large objects thrown into the air
F5	258–317 miles (416–510 km) an hour	catastrophic	• houses lifted off foundations and carried considerable distances before disintegrating • cars and other large objects fly through the air in excess of 300 feet (90 m) • steel reinforced concrete structures badly damaged

DISASTER FILE
The Super Outbreak

WHAT	The largest tornado outbreak ever recorded
WHERE	Across 11 states throughout the U.S.
WHEN	April 3–4, 1974
FUJITA SCALE	Mostly F5 and F4

The Super Outbreak of 1974 involved 148 tornadoes. This outbreak also had the most violent tornadoes. There were six F5 tornadoes and 24 F4 tornadoes. The outbreak lasted around 18 hours. During this time, 315 people were killed and more than 5,000 injured.

Why did it happen?

The Super Outbreak occurred at the end of a very strong **La Niña**. La Niña is a weather condition that can wreak havoc. When it occurs, it affects weather all around the world. During a La Niña, the Pacific Ocean experiences unusually cold temperatures, which can create a large number of supercell thunderstorms. All of the Super Outbreak tornadoes grew within supercell thunderstorms. They had a lot of warm, humid air and air movement to feed on. Conditions were perfect for the Super Outbreak to occur.

The first F5 tornado touched down in Ohio.

Counting the cost

The states that were hardest hit were Alabama, Kentucky, and Ohio. The first F5 tornado struck in Ohio. It ripped through Xenia, destroying more than 25 percent of the city. It killed 33 people and left 1,150 people injured. Five more F5s followed this first one. They struck in Ohio again, Alabama, Kentucky, and Indiana. At the height of this tornado outbreak, 15 tornadoes were on the ground at the same time. The outbreak finally ended in the early hours of the morning on April 4.

Think about it

The average lifetime of most tornadoes is two to three minutes. Strong tornadoes last about eight minutes. Violent tornado events can last up to 25 minutes and, in exceptional cases, may last more than three hours. The Super Outbreak lasted 18 hours total, making it the largest tornado outbreak ever recorded.

The walls on one side of this house were torn off by one of the Ohio tornadoes.

Storm chasers and spotters

One of the best ways to learn about tornadoes is to study them close-up. This might sound scary but scientists, storm chasers, and storm spotters find tornadoes fascinating. They know that there is much to be learned from studying them.

Storm chasers

Storm chasers chase tornadoes as a hobby. Serious storm chasers are usually the first on the scene. They photograph the tornado as it approaches and write reports about what they have seen. These can be very useful to meteorologists. Storm chasers can offer assistance after the storm as well. Many have first aid qualifications and carry rescue equipment with them.

Storm chasers are often the first on the scene once a tornado is spotted.

Storm spotters

Storm spotters are different than chasers. They are more like amateur meteorologists who watch storms and tornado activity. Storm spotters study severe thunderstorms and track funnels. They collect information about supercells and funnels and often report this information to meteorologists.

It is very important that chasers and spotters are aware of the dangers and know what they are doing. Tornadoes can be very unpredictable. The storms that form tornadoes can be enough to cause damage on their own. Untrained people can find themselves suddenly caught in the middle of severe weather. Serious spotters and chasers are skilled and take steps to be as safe as possible.

Professional storm chasers travel with a lot of useful equipment.

Disaster relief

After a tornado has struck, there is much to be done. The first step is to rescue any survivors. People and pets can be trapped underneath debris from a tornado. Areas are set up where relief can be provided to victims. People who have suffered the effects of a tornado may need more than medical attention. They might need clothing, shelter, food, and fresh water.

After relief efforts have been established, workers can assess the damage and begin cleaning up. Dangerously damaged structures need to be demolished. Finally, rebuilding begins. The costs of rebuilding communities can be massive. This can place strain on the economy of the country and on its government. Sometimes, extensive damage attracts aid from other countries that wish to help.

Rescue workers investigate the damage and search for survivors.

Living with tornadoes

The best protection from tornadoes comes from early warnings. Using the best resources available, meteorologists can often give warnings up to 20 minutes before a tornado strikes. However, some tornadoes allow no warning at all.

Strong buildings can offer some protection but the safest place to be is underground or in a tornado shelter. Modern buildings located in tornado-prone areas usually have underground tornado shelters. In buildings where there is no underground area, gathering in the

Think about it

Tornadoes don't just affect people—they affect animals too. Pets are not allowed inside emergency shelters due to public health and safety concerns. Thinking ahead and making arrangements for your pets in case you are evacuated could save your pet's life.

Homes and buildings in tornado-prone areas usually have basements that offer shelter.

DISASTER FILES AT A GLANCE

The four tornadoes profiled in this book are record-breaking for different reasons. This graph shows their intensity and their death tolls.

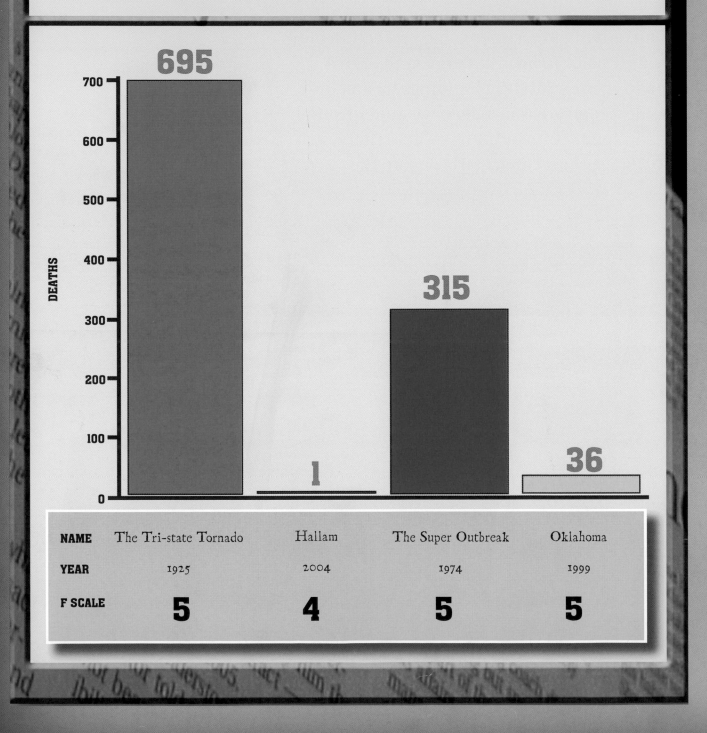

NAME	The Tri-state Tornado	Hallam	The Super Outbreak	Oklahoma
YEAR	1925	2004	1974	1999
F SCALE	5	4	5	5

Glossary

anemometer	instrument used to measure wind direction and speed
atmosphere	blanket of gases that surrounds Earth
condenses	when gas changes into liquid
debris	the remains of things that have been broken or destroyed
devastation	severe damage or destruction
Doppler radar	radar that locates and measures winds within a tornado
evaporates	when liquid changes into gas
Fujita scale	scale used for measuring the intensity of tornadoes
high pressure areas	large areas of cool, dry air
humid	contains a lot of water or water vapor
La Niña	abnormal cooling of surface waters in the tropical Pacific, which causes changes in weather patterns
low pressure areas	large areas of warm, humid air
meteorologists	scientists who study weather patterns
supercell thunderstorms	severe thunderstorms with deep, rotating updrafts
updraft	upward current of air
water vapor	water as a gas

Index

A
air pressure 20–21
anemometer 23
atmosphere 6, 10, 24

C
clouds 6, 10

D
debris 15, 20–21, 28
Doppler radar 12, 23
dust devils 19

F
Fujita scale 8, 12, 16, 23, 24
funnel 9, 14, 15, 16, 18–19, 20, 27
funnel cloud 10–11, 14–15

H
Hallam, Nebraska 16–17
high pressure 7

L
La Niña 24
low pressure 7

M
measuring 22–23
mesocyclone 10, 11, 16
meteorologist 8, 22–23, 26–27, 29

N
natural disasters, types of 4

O
Oklahoma City 12–13

P
predicting 22
protection 29

R
rebuilding 28
relief 28
rescue 28

S
storm chasers 26–27
storm spotters 26–27
supercell 11, 12, 14, 16, 24, 27
Super Outbreak 24–25

T
Tornado Alley 5, 8, 11, 16
tornado alert 22, 29
touchdown 14–15, 16, 22
Tri-state Tornado 8–9, 14, 21
twister 5

U
updraft 7, 10–11

W
waterspout 18
water vapor 6, 10
whirlwind 19
wind speed 12, 20